Promises
for Dad

Presented To:_____

Given By: _____

_____

Date:_____

I give thanks to my God for every
remembrance of you.
Philippians 1:3

Bible
Promises
for Dad

**BROADMAN
& HOLMAN
PUBLISHERS**

Nashville, Tennessee

Bible Promises for Dad
Copyright © 2003 by Broadman & Holman Publishers
All Rights Reserved

Broadman & Holman Publishers, Nashville, Tennessee
ISBN 0-8054-2733-3

Dewey Decimal Classification: 242.5
Subject Heading: God–Promises/Promises/Fathers

All Scripture verses are taken from the
HOLMAN CHRISTIAN STANDARD BIBLE®
Copyright © 1999, 2000, 2001, 2002, 2003
by Holman Bible Publishers

Printed in the United States
2 3 4 06 05 04 03

Contents

Promises for Everyday Life
Dealing with Stress 8
Desiring Discipline 14
Shooting for Balance 20
Making Good Decisions 26
Mastering Your Money 32

Promises for Your Family
The Gift of Children 40
The Covenant of Marriage 46
The Need for Leadership 52
The Pursuit of Legacy 58

Promises for Who You Are
A Man of Worth 66
A Man of Integrity 72
A Man on a Mission 78
A Man with a Plan 84
A Man of His Word 90

Promises for a Living Faith
A Heart for Worship 98
A Hunger for Prayer 104
A Burden for Others 110
A Need for Accountability 116
A Passion for Living 122

Promises for Everyday Life

When we try confining the Bible to the formality of Sunday mornings, we miss the Scripture's daily essence—the ability of God's truth to travel with us into staff meetings or onto the assembly line, to remain with us while we're pulling weeds in the vegetable garden or clearing snow from the front walk.

God's Word has been given to us not only to inspire us in expected settings, but also to infuse God's presence into places where we could easily ignore him—but where we need Him every hour, every minute, every day.

Dealing with Stress

I Don't Know If I Can Take Much More

God is our refuge and strength,
  a helper who is always found
  in times of trouble.
Therefore we will not be afraid,
  though the earth trembles
  and the mountains topple
  into the depths of the seas,
  though its waters roar and foam
  and the mountains quake with its turmoil.

Psalm 46:1-3

Trouble and distress terrify him: they over-
power him like a king poised for battle.

Job 15:24

Show us favor, LORD, show us favor,
    for we've had more than enough contempt.

Psalm 123:3

God, hear my cry;
    pay attention to my prayer.
I call to You from the ends of the earth
    when my heart is without strength.
Lead me to a rock that is high above me,
    for You have been a refuge for me,
    a strong tower in the face of the enemy.
I will live in Your tent forever,
    take refuge under the shelter of Your wings. . . .
Then I will continually sing of Your name,
    fulfilling my vows day by day.

Psalm 61:1-4, 8

This is the day the LORD has made;
    let us rejoice and be glad in it.
LORD, save us! LORD, please grant us success!

Psalm 118:24-25

Surely this is my suffering, and I must bear it.

Jeremiah 10:19b

For consider Him who endured such hostility from sinners against Himself, so that you won't grow weary and lose heart.

Hebrews 12:3

Stop your fighting—and know that I am God,
   exalted among the nations,
   exalted on the earth.

Psalm 46:10

He saw [the disciples] being battered as they rowed, because the wind was against them.
   Around three in the morning He came toward them walking on the sea, and wanted to pass by them. When they saw Him walking on the sea, they thought it was a ghost and cried out; for they all saw Him and were terrified.
   Immediately He spoke with them and said, "Have courage! It is I. Don't be afraid." Then He got into the boat with them, and the wind ceased.

Mark 6:48-51

Peace I leave with you. My peace I give to you. I do not give to you as the world gives. Your heart must not be troubled or fearful.

John 14:27

For the waywardness
   of the inexperienced will kill them,
   and the complacency of fools
   will destroy them.
But whoever listens to me will live securely
   and be free from the fear of danger.

Proverbs 1:32-33

The Bible is the one book to which any thoughtful man may go with any honest question of life or destiny and find the answer of God by honest searching.

–John Ruskin

For as the sufferings of Christ overflow to us, so our comfort overflows through Christ. If we are afflicted, it is for your comfort and salvation; if we are comforted, it is for your comfort, which is experienced in the endurance of the same sufferings that we suffer. . . .

For we don't want you to be unaware, brothers, of our affliction that took place in the province of Asia: we were completely over-whelmed—beyond our strength—so that we even despaired of life. However, we personally had a death sentence within ourselves so that we would not trust in ourselves, but in God who raises the dead.

He has delivered us from such a terrible death, and He will deliver us; we have placed our hope in Him that He will deliver us again.

2 Corinthians 1:5-6, 8-10

Dealing with Stress

Therefore don't worry about tomorrow, because tomorrow will worry about itself. Each day has enough trouble of its own.

Matthew 6:34

But as for you, keep a clear head about everything, endure hardship, do the work of an evangelist, fulfill your ministry.

2 Timothy 4:5

Share in suffering as a good soldier of Christ.

2 Timothy 2:3

Strengthen your tired hands and weakened knees, and make straight paths for your feet, so that what is lame may not be dislocated, but healed instead.

Hebrews 12:12-13

Say to the faint-hearted:
   "Be strong; do not fear!"

Isaiah 35:4a

Desiring Discipline

I Need to Finish What I've Started

For this very reason, make every effort to supplement your faith with goodness, goodness with knowledge, knowledge with self-control, self-control with endurance, endurance with godliness, godliness with brotherly affection, and brotherly affection with love. For if these qualities are yours and are increasing, they will keep you from being useless or unfruitful in the knowledge of our Lord Jesus Christ.

2 Peter 1:5-8

Patience is better than power,
   and controlling one's temper,
   than capturing a city.

Proverbs 16:32

For when we were in the flesh, the sinful passions operated through the law in every part of us and bore fruit for death.

But now we have been released from the law, since we have died to what held us, so that we may serve in the new way of the Spirit and not in the old letter of the law.

Romans 7:5-6

Therefore, get your minds ready for action, being self-disciplined, and set your hope completely on the grace to be brought to you at the revelation of Jesus Christ.

As obedient children, do not be conformed to the desires of your former ignorance but, as the One who called you is holy, you also are to be holy in all your conduct; for it is written, "Be holy, because I am holy."

1 Peter 1:13-16

LORD, You are our Father;
we are the clay, and You are our potter;
we all are the work of Your hand.

Isaiah 64:8

Christ has liberated us into freedom.
Therefore stand firm and don't submit again to
a yoke of slavery.

Galatians 5:1

I will instruct you and show you the way to go;
with My eye on you, I will give counsel.
Do not be like a horse or mule,
without understanding,
that must be controlled with bit and bridle,
or else it will not come near you.
Many pains come to the wicked,
but the one who trusts in the LORD
will have faithful love surrounding him.

Psalm 32:8-10

I love those who love me,
and those who search for me find me.

Proverbs 8:17

So then, brothers, we are not obligated to the flesh to live according to the flesh, for if you live according to the flesh, you are going to die. But if by the Spirit you put to death the deeds of the body, you will live.

Romans 8:12-13

But endurance must do its complete work, so that you may be mature and complete, lacking nothing.

James 1:4

Scholars may quote Plato in their studies, but the hearts of millions will quote the Bible at their daily toil, and draw strength from its inspiration, as the meadows draw it from the brook.

–M. Daniel Conway

Endure it as discipline: God is dealing with you as sons. For what son is there whom a father does not discipline? But if you are without discipline—which all receive—then you are illegitimate children and not sons.

Furthermore, we had natural fathers discipline us, and we respected them. Shouldn't we submit even more to the Father of spirits and live?

For they disciplined us for a short time based on what seemed good to them, but He does it for our benefit, so that we can share His holiness.

No discipline seems enjoyable at the time, but painful. Later on, however, it yields the fruit of peace and righteousness to those who have been trained by it.

Hebrews 12:7-11

Desiring Discipline

If anyone wants to come with Me, he must deny himself, take up his cross daily, and follow Me. For whoever wants to save his life will lose it, but whoever loses his life because of Me will save it. What is a man benefited if he gains the whole world, yet loses or forfeits himself?

Luke 9:23-25

But the fruit of the Spirit is love, joy, peace, patience, kindness, goodness, faith, gentleness, self-control. Against such things there is no law.

Now those who belong to Christ Jesus have crucified the flesh with its passions and desires. If we live by the Spirit, we must also follow the Spirit.

Galatians 5:22-25

Be sober! Be on the alert! Your adversary the Devil is prowling around like a roaring lion, looking for anyone he can devour.

Resist him, firm in the faith, knowing that the same sufferings are being experienced by your brothers in the world.

1 Peter 5:8-9

Shooting for Balance

Am I All Work and No Play?

Remember to dedicate the Sabbath day:
You are to labor six days and do all your work,
but the seventh day is a Sabbath to the LORD
your God. . . . For the LORD made the heavens
and the earth, the sea, and everything in them
in six days; then He rested on the seventh day.
Therefore the LORD blessed the Sabbath day
and declared it holy.

Exodus 20:8-10a, 11

Do not lack diligence; be fervent in spirit; serve the Lord.

Romans 12:11

Now we command and exhort such people, by the Lord Jesus Christ, that quietly working, they may eat their own bread. Brothers, do not grow weary in doing good.

2 Thessalonians 3:12-13

But we encourage you, brothers, to do so even more, to seek to lead a quiet life, to mind your own business, and to work with your own hands, as we commanded you, so that you may walk properly in the presence of outsiders and not be dependent on anyone.

1 Thessalonians 4:10b-12

And whatever you do, in word or in deed, do everything in the name of the Lord Jesus, giving thanks to God the Father through Him.

Colossians 3:17

What profit does the worker gain when he struggles? I see the business that God gives people to keep them busy. He has arranged everything appropriately in its time and has also put forever in their hearts. Still no one can discover the accomplishment God has accomplished from beginning to end.

I know nothing is better for anyone than to rejoice and to accomplish good with their lives. Also, it is God's gift whenever anyone eats, drinks, and experiences good in all his struggle.

Ecclesiastes 3:9-13

Therefore, whether you eat or drink, or whatever you do, do everything for God's glory.

1 Corinthians 10:31

You are to conduct yourselves in reverence during this time of temporary residence. For you know that you were redeemed from your empty way of life inherited from the fathers, not with perishable things, like silver or gold, but with the precious blood of Christ.

1 Peter 1:17b-19a

Now the end of all things is near; therefore, be clear-headed and disciplined for prayer. . . . Based on the gift they have received, everyone should use it to serve others, as good managers of the varied grace of God. If anyone speaks, his speech should be like the oracles of God; if anyone serves, his service should be from the strength God provides, so that in everything God may be glorified through Jesus Christ. To Him belong the glory and the power forever.

1 Peter 4:7, 10-11

The Bible goes equally to the cottage of the peasant and the palace of the king. It enters men's closets, directs their conduct, and mingles in all the grief and cheerfulness of life.

—Theodore Parker

*P*romises for Everyday Life

Everything has its appointed hour,
   every matter its time under the heavens:
   a time to give birth and a time to die;
   a time to plant
      and a time to uproot what is planted;
   a time to kill and a time to heal;
   a time to tear down and a time to build up;
   a time to weep and a time to laugh;
   a time to mourn and a time to dance;
   a time to throw stones away
      and a time to gather stones;
   a time to embrace and a time
      to keep one's distance from embracing;
   a time to search and a time to count as lost;
   a time to keep and a time to throw away;
   a time to tear and a time to sew;
   a time to be silent and a time to speak;
   a time to love and a time to hate;
   a time for war and a time for peace.

Ecclesiastes 3:1-8

Shooting for Balance

Be in agreement with one another. Do not be proud; instead, associate with the humble. Do not be wise in your own estimation. Do not repay anyone evil for evil. Try to do what is honorable in everyone's eyes. If possible, on your part, live at peace with everyone.

Romans 12:16-18

For if anyone considers himself to be something when he is nothing, he is deceiving himself. But each person should examine his own work, and then he will have a reason for boasting in himself alone, and not in respect to someone else. For each person will have to carry his own load.

Galatians 6:3-5

If anyone thinks he is religious, without controlling his tongue but deceiving his heart, his religion is useless. Pure and undefiled religion before our God and Father is this: to look after orphans and widows in their distress and to keep oneself unstained by the world.

James 1:26-27

Making Good Decisions

Sometimes I Just Don't Know What to Do

Now if any of you lacks wisdom, he should ask God, who gives to all generously and without criticizing, and it will be given to him.

But let him ask in faith without doubting. For the doubter is like the surging sea, driven and tossed by the wind. That person should not expect to receive anything from the Lord. An indecisive man is unstable in all his ways.

James 1:5-8

Brothers, don't be childish in your thinking,
but be infants in evil and adult in your thinking.
1 Corinthians 14:20

Trust in the LORD with all your heart,
   and do not rely on your own understanding;
   think about Him in all your ways,
   and He will guide you on the right paths.
Don't consider yourself to be wise;
   fear the Lord and turn away from evil.
Proverbs 3:5-7

Pay careful attention, then, to how you walk—
not as unwise people but as wise—making the
most of the time, because the days are evil.
So don't be foolish, but understand what the
Lord's will is.
Ephesians 5:15-17

Do not be conformed to this age, but be
transformed by the renewing of your mind, so
that you may discern what is the good, pleasing,
and perfect will of God.
Romans 12:2

You teach me wisdom deep within.

Psalm 51:6b

But be doers of the word and not hearers only, deceiving yourselves. Because if anyone is a hearer of the word and not a doer, he is like a man looking at his own face in a mirror; for he looks at himself, goes away, and right away forgets what kind of man he was.

But the one who looks intently into the perfect law of freedom and perseveres in it, and is not a forgetful hearer but a doer who acts—this person will be blessed in what he does.

James 1:22-25

The Spirit of the LORD will rest on Him—
a Spirit of wisdom and understanding,
a Spirit of counsel and strength, a Spirit
of knowledge and of the fear of the LORD.

Isaiah 11:2

Then you will understand righteousness,
justice, and integrity—every good path.

Proverbs 2:9

For wisdom will enter your heart,
  and knowledge will delight your soul.
Discretion will watch over you,
  and understanding will guard you.

Proverbs 2:10-11

Wisdom is better than weapons of war.

Ecclesiastes 9:18a

*The real influence of the Bible cannot
be measured. It is reckoned only in
terms of hearts that have been lifted
up, decisions that have been changed,
men and women who, in response to
its impervious demands, have done
justice and loved kindness and
walked humbly with their God.*

–J. Carter Swaim

My son, if you accept my words
  and store up my commands within you,
  listening closely to wisdom
  and directing your heart to understanding;
  furthermore, if you call out to insight
  and lift your voice to understanding,
  if you seek it like silver
  and search for it like hidden treasure,
  then you will understand the fear of the LORD
  and discover the knowledge of God.
For the LORD gives wisdom;
  from His mouth come
  knowledge and understanding.
He stores up success for the upright;
  He is a shield for those
  who live with integrity
  so that He may guard the paths of justice
  and protect the way of His loyal followers.

Proverbs 2:1-8

Making Good Decisions

Now everyone who lives on milk is inexperienced with the message about righteousness, because he is an infant. But solid food is for the mature—for those whose senses have been trained to distinguish between good and evil.

Hebrews 5:13-14

This also comes from the LORD of Hosts.
    He gives wonderful advice;
    He gives great wisdom.

Isaiah 28:29

He gives wisdom to the wise and knowledge
    to those who have understanding.
He reveals the deep and hidden things;
    He knows what is in the darkness,
    and light dwells with Him.
I offer thanks and praise to You,
    God of my fathers, because You
    have given me wisdom and power.
And now You have let me know
    what we asked of You.

Daniel 2:21b-23a

Mastering your Money

How Well Am I Handling My Finances?

Instruct those who are rich in the present age not to be arrogant or to set their hope on the uncertainty of wealth, but on God, who richly provides us with all things to enjoy.

Instruct them to do good, to be rich in good works, to be generous, willing to share, storing up for themselves a good foundation for the age to come, so that they may take hold of life that is real.

1 Timothy 6:17-19

One who loves money is never satisfied with money, and whoever loves wealth is never satisfied with his income.

Ecclesiastes 5:10a

For we brought nothing into the world, and we can take nothing out. But if we have food and clothing, we will be content with these.
But those who want to be rich fall into temptation, a trap, and many foolish and harmful desires, which plunge people into ruin and destruction. For the love of money is a root of all kinds of evil, and by craving it, some have wandered away from the faith and pierced themselves with many pains.

1 Timothy 6:7-10

Your life should be free from the love of money. Be satisfied with what you have.

Hebrews 13:5a

A faithful man will have many blessings.

Proverbs 28:20a

Honor the LORD with your possessions and
    with the first produce of your entire harvest;
then your barns will be completely filled,
    and your vats will overflow with new wine.

Proverbs 3:9-10

"Bring all the tithe to the treasure house so
it may be food in My house. Prove Me in this
matter," says the LORD of Hosts. "See if I will
not open for you the gates of heaven. I will pour
out blessing for you until there is no more room
for it, and I will rebuke for you the devourer
so that it does not ruin the fruit of the ground
and that the vine in the field will not fail to
bear for you. Then all the nations will declare
you as fortunate, for you will be a land of joy."

Malachi 3:10-12

Give, and it will be given to you; a good
measure, pressed down, shaken together, and
running over will be poured into your lap.
For with the measure that you use, it will
be measured back to you.

Luke 6:38

Remember this: the person who sows sparingly will also reap sparingly, and the person who sows generously will also reap generously. Each person should do as he has decided in his heart—not out of regret or out of necessity, for God loves a cheerful giver. And God is able to make every grace overflow to you, so that in every way, always having everything you need, you may excel in every good work.

2 Corinthians 9:6-8

Most people are bothered by those passages in Scripture which they cannot understand; but as for me, I always noticed that the passages in Scripture which trouble me most are those which I do understand.

—Mark Twain

Don't collect for yourselves treasures on earth, where moth and rust destroy and where thieves break in and steal.

But collect for yourselves treasures in heaven, where neither moth nor rust destroys and where thieves don't break in and steal. For where your treasure is, there your heart will be also.

The eye is the lamp of the body. If your eye is generous, your whole body will be full of light. But if your eye is stingy, your whole body will be full of darkness. So if the light within you is darkness—how deep is that darkness!

No one can be a slave of two masters, since either he will hate one and love the other, or be devoted to one and despise the other. You cannot be slaves of God and of money.

Matthew 6:19-24

Pay your obligations to everyone: taxes to those you owe taxes, tolls to those you owe tolls, respect to those you owe respect, and honor to those you owe honor.

Romans 13:7

Better a poor man who lives with integrity than a rich man who distorts right and wrong.

Proverbs 28:6

Why does a fool have money in his hand with no intention of buying wisdom?

Proverbs 17:16

A good name is to be chosen over great wealth; favor is better than silver and gold.

Proverbs 22:1

Don't work for the food that perishes but for the food that lasts for eternal life, which the Son of Man will give you, because on Him God the Father has set His seal of approval.

John 6:27

Promises for your Family

As fathers—the spiritual leaders of our homes—our duties and responsibilities run a lot deeper than repairing leaky faucets and changing light bulbs. People's lives are dependent on our leadership, in need of our discretion and judgment, weakened without our prayers.

So the Bible is more than God's love letter to us. It is our guidebook to what love looks like in the eyes and actions of a husband, what compassion feels like around the shoulders of a child. We are men charged with people's futures, and we need God's help to do it well.

The Gift of Children

I Hope They Know How Much I Love Them

Sons are indeed a heritage from the LORD,
  children, a reward.
Like arrows in the hand of a warrior
  are the sons born in one's youth.
Happy is the man
  who has filled his quiver with them.
Such men will never be put to shame
  when they speak with their enemies
  at the city gate.

Psalm 127:3-5

Come, children, listen to me;
    I will teach you the fear of the LORD.
Who is the man who delights in life,
    loving a long life to enjoy what is good?
Keep your tongue from evil
    and your lips from deceitful speech.
Turn away from evil and do good;
    seek peace and pursue it.

Psalm 34:11-14

In the fear of the LORD one has strong
    confidence and his children have a refuge.

Proverbs 14:26

He protects his flock like a shepherd;
    He gathers the lambs in His arms,
    and carries them in the fold of His garment.

Isaiah 40:11a

For I have chosen him so that he will command his children and his house after him to keep the way of the LORD by doing what is right and just.

Genesis 18:19a

Discipline your son, and he will give you
   comfort; he will also give you delight.
Proverbs 29:17

Do not despise the LORD's instruction,
   my son, and do not loathe His discipline;
   for the LORD disciplines the one He loves,
   just as a father, the son he delights in.
Proverbs 3:11-12

What man among you, if his son asks him
for bread, will give him a stone? Or if he asks
for a fish, will give him a snake?
   If you then, who are evil, know how to give
good gifts to your children, how much more
will your Father in heaven give good things to
those who ask Him!
Matthew 7:9-11

Fathers, don't stir up anger in your children,
but bring them up in the training and instruction of the Lord.
Ephesians 6:4

The Gift of Children

The one who will not use the rod
hates his son, but the one who loves him
disciplines him diligently.

Proverbs 13:24

There are thorns and snares
on the path of the crooked; the one
who guards himself stays far from them.
Teach a youth about the way he should go;
even when he is old he will not depart from it.

Proverbs 22:5-6

*If there is anything in my thoughts or
style to commend, the credit is due to
my parents for instilling in me an
early love of the Scriptures. If we abide
by the principles taught there, our
country will go on prospering.*

–Daniel Webster

Promises for Your Family

My people, hear my instruction;
   listen to what I say.
I will declare wise sayings;
   I will speak mysteries from the past—
   things we have heard and known
   and that our fathers have passed down to us.
We must not hide them from their children,
   but must tell a future generation
   the praises of the LORD, His might,
   and the wonderful works
   He has performed. . . .
   so that a future generation—
   children yet to be born—might know.
They were to rise and tell their children
   so that they might
   put their confidence in God
   and not forget God's works,
   but keep His commandments.

Psalm 78:1-4, 6-7

The Gift of Children

See that you don't look down on one of these little ones, because I tell you that in heaven their angels continually view the face of My Father in heaven. . . .

What do you think? If a man has 100 sheep, and one of them goes astray, won't he leave the 99 on the hillside, and go and search for the stray? And if he finds it, I assure you: He rejoices over that sheep more than over the 99 that did not go astray. In the same way, it is not the will of your Father in heaven that one of these little ones perish.

Matthew 18:10, 12-14

Whoever welcomes one little child such as this in My name welcomes Me.

Mark 9:37a

I am not seeking what is yours, but you. For children are not obligated to save up for their parents, but parents for their children. I will most gladly spend and be spent for you.

2 Corinthians 12:14b-15a

The Covenant of Marriage

*When You Gave Me a Wife,
You Gave Me a Friend*

The man said: "This one, at last, is bone of my bone, and flesh of my flesh; this one will be called woman, for she was taken from man."

This is why a man leaves his father and mother and bonds with his wife, and they become one flesh.

Genesis 2:23-24

Husbands, love your wives, just as also Christ loved the church and gave Himself for her, to make her holy, cleansing her in the washing of water by the word.

He did this to present the church to Himself in splendor, without spot or wrinkle or any such thing, but holy and blameless.

Ephesians 5:25-27

Husbands, in the same way, live with your wives with understanding of their weaker nature yet showing them honor as co-heirs of the grace of life, so that your prayers will not be hindered.

1 Peter 3:7

With all humility and gentleness, with patience, accepting one another in love.

Ephesians 4:2

A man who finds a wife finds a good thing and obtains favor from the LORD.

Proverbs 18:22

A husband should fulfill his marital duty to his wife, and likewise a wife to her husband.

A wife does not have authority over her own body, but her husband does. Equally, a husband does not have authority over his own body, but his wife does.

1 Corinthians 7:3-4

I imposed a covenant on my eyes.
  How then could I concentrate
  my attention on a young lady?
For what portion would one have
  from God above, or what inheritance
  from the Almighty on high?
Would it not bring calamity to the unjust
  and misfortune for evildoers?
Does He not see my ways
  and number all my steps?

Job 31:1-4

Marriage must be respected by all, and the marriage bed kept undefiled.

Hebrews 13:4a

The Covenant of Marriage

Drink water from your own cistern,
   water flowing from your own well.
Should your springs flow in the streets,
   streams of water in the public squares?
They should be for you alone
   and not for you to share with strangers.
Let your fountain be blessed,
   and take pleasure in the wife of your youth.
A loving doe, a graceful fawn—
   let her breasts always satisfy you;
   be lost in her love forever.

Proverbs 5:15-19

*The Word of Scripture should never
stop sounding in your ears and working in you all day long, just like the
words of someone you love.*

—Dietrich Bonhoeffer

Wives, submit to your own husbands as to the Lord, for the husband is head of the wife as also Christ is head of the church. He is the Savior of the body. . . .

Husbands should love their wives as their own bodies. He who loves his wife loves himself. For no one ever hates his own flesh, but provides and cares for it, just as Christ does for the church, since we are members of His body.

For this reason a man will leave his father and mother and be joined to his wife, and the two will become one flesh.

This mystery is profound, but I am talking about Christ and the church. To sum up, each one of you is to love his wife as himself, and the wife is to respect her husband.

Ephesians 5:22-23, 28-33

The Covenant of Marriage

How beautiful you are, my darling.
  How very beautiful!
  Your eyes are doves.

Song of Songs 1:15

Like a lily among thorns,
  so is my darling among the young women.

Song of Songs 2:2

Love's flames are fiery flames—
  the fiercest of all.
Mighty waters cannot extinguish love;
  rivers cannot sweep it away.

Song of Songs 8:6b-7a

Arise, my darling.
  Come away, my beautiful one.

Song of Songs 2:13b

You have captured my heart
  with one glance of your eyes.

Song of Songs 4:9b

The Need for Leadership

I Want to Be Strong for My Family

I will lead the blind
   by a way they did not know;
   I will guide them on paths
   they have not known.
I will turn darkness to light in front of them,
   and rough places into level ground.
This is what I will do for them,
   and I will not forsake them.

Isaiah 42:16

I thought, "Age should speak,
   and maturity should teach wisdom."
But indeed the Spirit is in a person;
   the breath of the Almighty
   gives people understanding.
The old are not necessarily wise, nor do elders
   necessarily understand what is just.
Therefore, I say, listen to me
   I will declare what I know.

Job 32:7-10a

When He set up a limit for the rain
   and a path for the thunder and lightning,
   then He considered wisdom and evaluated it;
   He established it and examined it.
And He told man,
   "Look! The fear of the Lord—that is wisdom;
   to turn from evil—that is understanding."

Job 28:26-28

When pride comes, disgrace follows,
   but with humility comes wisdom.
The integrity of the upright guides them.

Proverbs 11:2-3a

Promises for Your Family

I pray that the God of our Lord Jesus Christ, the glorious Father, would give you a spirit of wisdom and revelation in the knowledge of Him. I pray that the eyes of your heart may be enlightened so you may know what is the hope of His calling, what are the glorious riches of His inheritance among the saints, and what is the immeasurable greatness of His power to us who believe, according to the working of His vast strength.

Ephesians 1:17-19

When the Spirit of truth comes, He will guide you into all the truth. For He will not speak on His own, but He will speak whatever He hears. He will also declare to you what is to come. He will glorify Me, because He will take from what is Mine and declare it to you.

John 16:13-14

Now we have not received the spirit of the world, but the Spirit who is from God, in order to know what has been freely given us by God.

1 Corinthians 2:12

Send Your light and Your truth;
   let them lead me. Let them bring me to
   Your holy mountain, to Your dwelling place.
                              Psalm 43:3

Don't those who plan evil go astray?
   But those who plan good
   find loyalty and faithfulness.
                              Proverbs 14:22

A man's heart plans his way,
   but the LORD determines his steps.
                              Proverbs 16:9

The man of one book is always
formidable; but when that book is
the Bible, he is irresistible.
                              —William M. Taylor

If you get rid of the yoke from those
   around you, the finger-pointing
   and malicious speaking,
   and if you offer yourself to the hungry,
   and satisfy the afflicted one,
   then your light will shine
   in the darkness, and your night
   will be like noonday.
The LORD will always lead you,
   satisfy you in a parched land,
   and strengthen your bones.
You will be like a watered garden
   and like a spring whose waters never run dry.
You will rebuild the ancient ruins;
   you will restore the foundations
   laid long ago; you will be called
   the repairer of broken walls,
   the restorer of streets where people live.

Isaiah 58:9b-12

The Need for Leadership

An overseer, therefore, must be above reproach, the husband of one wife, self-controlled, sensible, respectable, hospitable, an able teacher, not addicted to wine, not a bully but gentle, not quarrelsome, not greedy—one who manages his own household competently, having his children under control with all dignity.

1 Timothy 3:2-4

He must hold to the faithful message as taught, so that he will be able both to encourage with sound teaching and to refute those who contradict it.

Titus 1:9

The gate is wide and the road is broad that leads to destruction, and there are many who go through it. How narrow is the gate and difficult the road that leads to life; and few find it.

Matthew 7:13b-14

I labor for this, striving with His strength that works powerfully in me.

Colossians 1:29

The Pursuit of Legacy

May I Be Known for Knowing You

From eternity to eternity
    the LORD's faithful love
    is toward those who fear Him,
    and His righteousness
    toward the grandchildren
    of those who keep His covenant,
    who remember to observe His instructions.

Psalm 103:17-18

A good man leaves an inheritance
to his grandchildren,
but the sinner's wealth
is stored up for the righteous.

Proverbs 13:22

The one who lives
with integrity is righteous,
his children who come
after him will be happy.

Proverbs 20:7

Only take care and diligently watch yourselves so you don't forget the things your eyes
have seen, so they don't slip from your mind
all the days of your life. Teach them to your
children and your grandchildren.

Deuteronomy 4:9

Therefore, be imitators of God, as dearly
loved children.

Ephesians 5:1

Promises for Your Family

I pray that you, being rooted and firmly established in love, may be able to comprehend with all the saints what is the breadth and width, height and depth, and to know the Messiah's love that surpasses knowledge, so you may be filled with all the fullness of God.

Ephesians 3:17b-19

Listen, my sons, to a father's discipline,
   and pay attention
   so that you may gain understanding,
   for I am giving you good instruction.
   Don't abandon my teaching.
When I was a son with my father,
   tender and precious to my mother,
   he taught me and said:
   "Your heart must hold on to my words.
   Keep my commands and live."

Proverbs 4:1-4

For it is not a word that has no meaning for you; rather it is your life.

Deuteronomy 32:47a

The Pursuit of Legacy

My son, if your heart is wise,
   my heart will indeed rejoice.
My innermost being will cheer
   when your lips say what is right.
Don't be jealous of sinners;
   instead, always fear the LORD.
For then you will have a future,
   and your hope will never fade.

Proverbs 23:15-18

*Do you know a book you are willing
to put under your head when you lay
dying? That is the book you want to
study while you are living. There is
but one such Book in the world.*

—Joseph Cook

Promises for Your Family

My son, pay attention to my words;
   listen closely to my sayings.
Don't lose sight of them;
   keep them within your heart.
For they are life to those who find them,
   and health to one's whole body.
Guard your heart above all else,
   for it is the source of life.
Don't let your mouth speak dishonestly,
   and don't let your lips talk deviously.
Let your eyes look forward;
   fix your gaze straight ahead.
Carefully consider the path for your feet,
   and all your ways will be established.
Don't turn to the right or to the left;
   keep your feet away from evil.

Proverbs 4:20-27

The Pursuit of Legacy

May the LORD bless you and protect you;
  may the LORD make His face shine on you
  and be gracious to you;
  may the LORD show His face to you
  and give you peace.

Numbers 6:24-26

May the LORD add to your numbers,
  both yours and your children's.
May you be blessed by the Lord,
  the Maker of heaven and earth.

Psalm 115:14-15

Go around Zion, encircle it; count its towers,
  note its ramparts; tour its citadels
  so that you can tell a future generation:
"This God, our God forever and ever—
  He will lead us eternally."

Psalm 48:12-14

Your servants' children will dwell securely,
  and their offspring will be
  established before You.

Psalm 102:28

Promises for Who you Are

Some dads are fathers in name only. And some of them, in fact, who have given so little to their families, still have a lot of nice stuff to show for it. Success has seemed to flow into their hands regardless of their relationships.

But others—like you—are deliberate dads, focused fathers, men who love their families well and pour importance into their role.

So keep your eyes on the God who offers true success through the path of faithfulness, obedience, devotion. Your brand of fatherhood, my friend, looks really good on you.

A Man of Worth

At Times, I Wonder How Much I Matter

The first man was from the earth and made of dust; the second man is from heaven.

Like the man made of dust, so are those who are made of dust; like the heavenly man, so are those who are heavenly.

And just as we have borne the image of the man made of dust, we will also bear the image of the heavenly man.

1 Corinthians 15:47-49

Do you not recognize for yourselves that Jesus Christ is in you?

2 Corinthians 13:5b

For in Him we live and move and exist, as even some of your own poets have said, "For we are also His offspring."

Acts 17:28

Therefore if anyone is in Christ, there is a new creation; old things have passed away, and look, new things have come.

2 Corinthians 5:17

You took off your former way of life, the old man that is corrupted by deceitful desires; you are being renewed in the spirit of your minds; you put on the new man, the one created according to God's likeness in righteousness and purity of the truth.

Ephesians 4:22-24

Brothers, consider your calling: not many
are wise from a human perspective, not many
powerful, not many of noble birth.

Instead, God has chosen the world's foolish
things to shame the wise, and God has chosen
the world's weak things to shame the strong.

God has chosen the world's insignificant
and despised things—the things viewed as
nothing—so He might bring to nothing the
things that are viewed as something, so that
no one can boast in His presence.

But from Him you are in Christ Jesus, who
for us became wisdom from God, as well as
righteousness, sanctification, and redemption,
in order that, as it is written: "The one who
boasts must boast in the Lord."

1 Corinthians 1:26-31

Indeed, it was for my own welfare that I had
such great bitterness; but Your love has delivered me from the Pit of destruction, for You
have thrown all my sins behind Your back.

Isaiah 38:17

A Man of Worth

Who is a God like You,
   removing iniquity and forgiving transgression
   for the remnant of His inheritance?
Who does not hold on to His anger forever,
   because He delights in faithful love.
Who will again have compassion on us;
   who will vanquish our iniquities.

Micah 7:18-19a

He made the One who did not know sin to
be sin for us, so that we might become the
righteousness of God in Him.

2 Corinthians 5:21

*All that I am, I owe to Jesus Christ,
revealed to me in his divine Book,
the Bible.*

–David Livingstone

Promises for Who You Are

When I observe Your heavens,
   the work of Your fingers,
   the moon and the stars,
   which You set in place,
   what is man, that You remember him,
   the son of man, that You look after him?
You made him little less than God
   and crowned him with glory and honor.
You made him lord
   over the works of Your hands;
   You put everything under his feet:
   all the sheep and oxen,
   as well as animals in the wild,
   birds of the sky, and fish of the sea
   passing through the currents of the seas.
O LORD, our Lord,
   how magnificent is Your name
   throughout the earth!

Psalm 8:3-9

A Man of Worth

He has not dealt with us as our sins deserve
   or repaid us according to our offenses.
For as high as the heavens are above the earth,
   so great is His faithful love
   toward those who fear Him.
As far as the east is from the west,
   so far has He removed
   our transgressions from us.

Psalm 103:10-12

How happy are those whose lawless acts are
forgiven and whose sins are covered!

Romans 4:7

Therefore, brothers, since we have boldness
to enter the sanctuary through the blood of
Jesus, by the new and living way that He has
inaugurated for us, through the curtain (that
is, His flesh); and since we have a great high
priest over the house of God, let us draw near
with a true heart in full assurance of faith, our
hearts sprinkled clean from an evil conscience
and our bodies washed in pure water.

Hebrews 10:19-22

A Man
of Integrity

Help Me Be the Person I Really Want to Be

I will pay attention to the way of integrity.
 When will You come to me?
I will live with integrity of heart in my house.
 I will not set anything godless before my eyes.
I hate the doing of transgression;
 it will not cling to me.
A devious heart will be far from me;
 I will not be involved with evil.

Psalm 101:2-4

A man who does not control his temper
is like a city whose wall is broken down.

Proverbs 25:28

A fool gives full vent to his anger,
but a wise man holds it in check.

Proverbs 29:11

A gossip goes around revealing a secret,
but the trustworthy keeps a confidence.

Proverbs 11:13

For we are His creation—created in Christ
Jesus for good works, which God prepared
ahead of time so that we should walk in them.

Ephesians 2:10

Righteousness guards people of integrity,
but wickedness undermines the sinner.

Proverbs 13:6

Dear friends, if our hearts do not condemn us we have confidence before God, and can receive whatever we ask from Him because we keep His commands and do what is pleasing in His sight.

1 John 3:21-22

For this is what love for God is: to keep His commands. Now His commands are not a burden.

1 John 5:3

For this is God's will, your sanctification: that you abstain from sexual immorality, so that each of you knows how to possess his own vessel in sanctification and honor, not with lustful desires, like the Gentiles who don't know God.

This means one must not transgress against and defraud his brother in this matter, because the Lord is an avenger of all these offenses, as we also previously told and warned you.

For God has not called us to impurity, but to sanctification.

1 Thessalonians 4:3-7

A Man of Integrity

For the one who wants to love life
   and to see good days
   must keep his tongue from evil
   and his lips from speaking deceit,
   and he must turn away
   from evil and do good.
He must seek peace and pursue it,
   because the eyes of the Lord
   are on the righteous
   and His ears are open to their request.

1 Peter 3:10-12a

When you have read the Bible,
you will know it is the Word of God,
because you will have found it the
key to your own heart, your own
happiness, and your own duty.

—Woodrow Wilson

Now in a large house there are not only gold and silver bowls, but also those of wood and earthenware, some for special use, some for ordinary. So if anyone purifies himself from these things, he will be a special instrument, set apart, useful to the Master, prepared for every good work.

Flee from youthful passions, and pursue righteousness, faith, love, and peace, along with those who call on the Lord from a pure heart. But reject foolish and ignorant disputes, knowing that they breed quarrels.

The Lord's slave must not quarrel, but must be gentle to everyone, able to teach, and patient, instructing his opponents with gentleness.

Perhaps God will grant them repentance to know the truth.

2 Timothy 2:20-25

A Man of Integrity

Walk as children of light—for the fruit of the light results in all goodness, righteousness, and truth—discerning what is pleasing to the Lord. Don't participate in the fruitless works of darkness, but instead, expose them. For it is shameful even to mention what is done by them in secret. Everything exposed by the light is made clear, for what makes everything clear is light.

Ephesians 5:8b-14a

Therefore, God's chosen ones, holy and loved, put on heartfelt compassion, kindness, humility, gentleness, and patience, accepting one another and forgiving one another if anyone has a complaint against another. Just as the Lord has forgiven you, so also you must forgive. Above all, put on love—the perfect bond of unity.

Colossians 3:12-14

Be alert, stand firm in the faith, be brave and strong. Your every action must be done with love.

1 Corinthians 16:13-14

A Man on a Mission

This Is What I Was Put on This Earth to Do

If I walk in the thick of danger,
    You will preserve my life
    from the anger of my enemies.
You will extend Your hand;
    Your right hand will save me.
The LORD will fulfill His purpose for me.
    LORD, Your love is eternal;
    do not abandon the work of Your hands.

Psalm 138:7-8

Make your own attitude that of Christ Jesus,
   who, existing in the form of God,
   did not consider equality with God
   as something to be used
   for His own advantage.
Instead He emptied Himself
   by assuming the form of a slave,
   taking on the likeness of men.
And when He had come as a man
   in His external form, He humbled Himself
   by becoming obedient to the point
   of death—even to death on a cross.
For this reason God also highly exalted Him
   and gave Him the name that is above
   every name, so that at the name of Jesus
   every knee should bow—of those who are
   in heaven and on earth and under the
   earth—and every tongue should confess
   that Jesus Christ is Lord, to the
   glory of God the Father.

Philippians 2:5-11

For me, living is Christ.

Philippians 1:21a

Promises for Who You Are

Dear friends, when the fiery ordeal arises among you to test you, don't be surprised by it, as if something unusual were happening to you.

Instead, as you share in the sufferings of the Messiah rejoice, so that you may also rejoice with great joy at the revelation of His glory.

If you are ridiculed for the name of Christ, you are blessed, because the Spirit of glory and of God rests on you.

1 Peter 4:12-14

In fact, all those who want to live a godly life in Christ Jesus will be persecuted.

2 Timothy 3:12

So don't be ashamed of the testimony about our Lord. . . . Instead, share in suffering for the gospel, relying on the power of God, who has saved us and called us with a holy calling, not according to our works, but according to His own purpose and grace, which was given to us in Christ Jesus before time began.

2 Timothy 1:8-9

A Man on a Mission

We know that all things work together for the good of those who love God: those who are called according to His purpose.

Romans 8:28

Many plans are in a man's heart,
  but the LORD's decree will prevail.

Proverbs 19:21

The Bible is to us what the star was to the wise men. But if we spend all our time in gazing upon it, observing its motions, and admiring its splendor without being led to Christ by it, the use of it will be lost to us.

—Thomas Adams

Promises for Who You Are

Get wisdom, get understanding;
  don't forget or turn away
  from the words of my mouth.
Don't abandon wisdom,
  and she will watch over you;
  love her, and she will guard you.
Wisdom is supreme—so get wisdom.
  And whatever else you get,
  get understanding.
Cherish her, and she will exalt you;
  if you embrace her,
  she will honor you.
She will place a garland
  of grace on your head;
  she will give you a crown of beauty. . .
When you walk,
  your steps will not be hindered;
  when you run, you will not stumble.

Proverbs 4:5-9, 12

A Man on a Mission

For this reason also, since the day we heard this, we haven't stopped praying for you.

We are asking that you may be filled with the knowledge of His will in all wisdom and spiritual understanding, so that you may walk worthy of the Lord, fully pleasing to Him, bearing fruit in every good work and growing in the knowledge of God. May you be strengthened with all power, according to His glorious might, for all endurance and patience, with joy giving thanks to the Father, who has enabled you to share in the saints' inheritance in the light.

Colossians 1:9-12

And in view of this, we always pray for you that our God will consider you worthy of His calling, and will—by His power—fulfill every desire for goodness and the work of faith, so that the name of our Lord Jesus will be glorified by you, and you by Him, according to the grace of our God and the Lord Jesus Christ.

2 Thessalonians 1:11-12

A Man
with a Plan

Lord, Show Me the Way You Want Me to Go

"For I know the plans I have for you," says the LORD, "wholesome plans and not harmful, to give you a future and hope.

"You will call to Me and come and pray to Me. Then I will listen to you. You will seek Me and find Me if you seek for Me with all your heart."

Jeremiah 29:11-13

Commit your activities to the LORD
and your plans will be achieved.

Proverbs 16:3

Plans fail when there is no counsel,
but with many advisers they succeed.

Proverbs 15:22

The counsel of the LORD stands forever,
the plans of His heart
from generation to generation.

Psalm 33:11

I know You can do anything;
no plan of Yours can be denied.

Job 42:2

May He give you what your heart desires
and fulfill your whole purpose.

Psalm 20:4

What the wicked dreads
will come upon him,
but what the righteous desires
will be given to him.

Proverbs 10:24

Not that I have already reached the goal or am
already fully mature, but I make every effort to
take hold of it because I also have been taken
hold of by Christ Jesus.

Brothers, I do not consider myself to have
taken hold of it. But one thing I do: forgetting
what is behind and reaching forward to what is
ahead, I pursue as my goal the prize promised
by God's heavenly call in Christ Jesus.

Philippians 3:12-14

For we know that if our earthly house, a tent,
is destroyed, we have a building from God,
a house not made with hands, eternal in the
heavens. . . . And the One who prepared us
for this very thing is God, who gave us the
Spirit as a down payment.

2 Corinthians 5:1, 5

A Man with a Plan

Though we are always confident and know that while we are at home in the body we are away from the Lord—for we walk by faith, not by sight—yet we are confident and satisfied to be out of the body and at home with the Lord. Therefore, whether we are at home or away, we make it our aim to be pleasing to Him.

2 Corinthians 5:6-9

For we are convinced that we have a clear conscience, wanting to conduct ourselves honorably in everything.

Hebrews 13:18b

The Word of God will stand a thousand readings. And he who has gone over it most frequently is the surest of finding new wonders there.

—James Hamilton

Promises for Who You Are

Commit your way to the LORD;
   trust in Him, and He will act,
   making your righteousness
   shine like the dawn,
   your justice like the noonday.
Be silent before the LORD
   and wait expectantly for Him;
   do not be agitated by one
   who prospers in his way,
   by the man who carries out evil plans.
Refrain from anger and give up your rage;
   do not be agitated—
   it can only bring harm.
For evildoers will be destroyed,
   but those who hope in the LORD
   will inherit the land.

Psalm 37:5-9

A Man with a Plan

The LORD makes poor and gives wealth;
  He humbles and He exalts.
He raises the poor from the dust
  and lifts the needy from the ash heap.
He seats them with noblemen
  and grants them a throne of honor.
For the foundations of the earth
  belong to the LORD;
  He has set the world on them.
He guards the feet of His devout followers,
  but the wicked are silenced in the darkness
  for it is not through strength
  that a man prevails.

1 Samuel 2:7-9

I am able to do all things through Him who
strengthens me.

Philippians 4:13

No wisdom, no understanding,
  and no counsel will prevail against the LORD.
A horse is prepared for the day of battle,
  but victory comes from the LORD.

Proverbs 21:30-31

A Man of His Word

Give Me a New Hunger for the Bible

I will meditate on Your precepts
  and think about Your ways.
I will delight in Your statutes;
  I will not forget Your word. . . .
Your statutes are the theme of my song
  during my earthly life.
I remember Your name in the night, LORD,
  and I keep Your law.
This is my practice: I obey Your precepts.

Psalm 119:15-16, 54-56

Every word of God is pure;
   He is a shield to those
   who take refuge in Him.

Proverbs 30:5

How happy are those whose way is blameless,
   who live according to the law of the LORD!
Happy are those who keep His decrees
   and seek Him with all their heart.

Psalm 119:1-2

For whatever was written before was
written for our instruction, so that through
our endurance and through the encouragement
of the Scriptures we may have hope.

Romans 15:4

Remember Your word to Your servant,
   through which You have given me hope.
This is my comfort in my affliction:
   Your promise has given me life.

Psalm 119:49-50

Promises for Who You Are

As for you, continue in what you have learned and firmly believed, knowing those from whom you learned, and that from childhood you have known the sacred Scriptures, which are able to instruct you for salvation through faith in Christ Jesus.

2 Timothy 3:14-15

The wise will be put to shame;
  they will be dismayed and snared.
They have rejected the word of the LORD,
  so what wisdom do they really have?

Jeremiah 8:9

I have Your decrees as a heritage forever;
  indeed, they are the joy of my heart.
I am resolved to obey Your statutes
  to the very end.

Psalm 119:111-112

Your word is completely pure,
  and Your servant loves it.

Psalm 119:140

A Man of His Word

LORD, Your word is forever;
   it is firmly fixed in heaven. . . .
They stand today in accordance with Your
   judgments, for all things are Your servants.
If Your instruction had not been my delight,
   I would have died in my affliction.
I will never forget Your precepts,
   for You have given me life through them. . . .
I have seen a limit to all perfection,
   but Your command is without limit.

Psalm 119:89, 91-93, 96

*God himself has condescended to
teach the way. For this very end he
came from heaven. And he hath
written it down in a book. O give
me that Book! At any price, give
me the Book of God!*

–John Wesley

The instruction of the LORD
  is perfect, reviving the soul;
  the testimony of the LORD is trustworthy,
  making the inexperienced wise.
The precepts of the LORD are right,
  making the heart glad;
  the commandment of the LORD is radiant,
  making the eyes light up.
The fear of the LORD is pure, enduring forever;
  the ordinances of the LORD
  are reliable and altogether righteous.
They are more desirable than gold—
  than an abundance of pure gold;
  and sweeter than honey—
  than honey dripping from the comb.
In addition, Your servant is warned by them;
  there is great reward in keeping them.

Psalm 19:7-11

A Man of His Word

I delight to do Your will, my God;
  Your instruction resides within me.

Psalm 40:8

Your decrees are my delight
  and my counselors.

Psalm 119:24

I rejoice in the way revealed by Your decrees
  as much as in all riches.

Psalm 119:14

Long ago I learned from Your decrees
  that You have established them forever.

Psalm 119:152

The entirety of Your word is truth,
  and all Your righteous judgments
  endure forever.

Psalm 119:160

Promises for a Living Faith

Little things: Making sure your family is in church on Sunday. Making sure the day doesn't start until you've met God in prayer. Making sure others have theirs before you get yours.

The Christian life begins with a big thing: Jesus Christ coming to earth, dying on a cross to forgive our sins, returning to life to make death a toothless enemy. But the Christian life bears fruit in the little things—the little things your children admire in you, the little things you add to an ordinary day, the little things you do that make your life a blessing to so many.

A Heart for Worship

I'll Praise You Today, I'll Praise You Forever

Better a day in Your courts
   than a thousand anywhere else.
I would rather be at the door
   of the house of my God
   than to live in the tents of the wicked.
For the LORD God is a sun and shield.
   The LORD gives grace and glory;
   He does not withhold the good
   from those who live with integrity.

Psalm 84:10-11

Come, let us worship and bow down;
  let us kneel before the LORD our Maker.
For He is our God, and we are the people
  of His pasture, the sheep under His care.

Psalm 95:6-7

We all went astray like sheep;
  we all have turned to our own way.
  and the LORD has punished Him
  for the iniquity of all of us.

Isaiah 53:6

For you know the grace of our Lord Jesus
Christ: although He was rich, for your sake He
became poor, so that by His poverty you might
become rich.

2 Corinthians 8:9

My salvation and glory depend on God;
  my strong rock, my refuge, is in God.
Trust in Him at all times, you people;
  pour out your hearts before Him.
God is our refuge.

Psalm 62:7-8

Promises for a Living Faith

Whom do I have in heaven but You?
    And I desire nothing on earth but You.
My flesh and my heart may fail,
    but God is the strength of my heart,
    my portion forever.

Psalm 73:25-26

God—His way is perfect;
    the word of the LORD is pure.
He is a shield to all
    who take refuge in Him.
For who is God besides the LORD?
    And who is a rock? Only our God.
God—He clothes me with strength
    and makes my way perfect.
He makes my feet like the feet of a deer
    and sets me securely on the heights.

Psalm 18:30-33

Clap your hands, all you peoples;
    shout to God with a jubilant cry.
For the LORD Most High is awe-inspiring,
    a great King over all the earth.

Psalm 47:1-2

A Heart for Worship

Shout triumphantly to the LORD, all the earth.
  Serve the LORD with gladness;
  come before Him with joyful songs.
Acknowledge that the LORD is God.
  He made us, and we are His—
  His people, the sheep of His pasture.
Enter His gates with thanksgiving
  and His courts with praise.
Give thanks to Him and praise His name.
  For the LORD is good, and His love is eternal;
  His faithfulness endures
  through all generations.

Psalm 100:1-5

*The Bible furnishes the only fitting
vehicle to express the thoughts that
overwhelm us when contemplating
the stellar universe.*

–O. M. Mitchell

Ascribe to the LORD,
  O families of the peoples,
  ascribe to the LORD glory and strength.
Ascribe to the LORD the glory due His name;
  bring an offering and come before Him.
Worship the LORD in His holy majesty;
  tremble before Him, all the earth.
The world is firmly established;
  it cannot be shaken.
Let the heavens be glad and the earth rejoice,
  and let them say among the nations,
  "The LORD is King!"
Let the sea and everything in it resound;
  let the fields and all that is in them exult.
Then the trees of the forest
  will shout for joy before the LORD,
  for He comes to judge the earth.

1 Chronicles 16:28-33

Let me experience Your faithful love
 in the morning, for I trust in You.
Reveal to me the way I should go,
 because I long for You.
Rescue me from my enemies, LORD;
 I come to You for protection.
Teach me to do Your will,
 for You are my God.
May Your gracious Spirit
 lead me on level ground.

Psalm 143:8-10

Now this is the confidence we have before
Him: whenever we ask anything according to
His will, He hears us. And if we know that He
hears whatever we ask, we know that we have
what we have asked Him for.

1 John 5:14-15

Keep asking, and it will be given to you. Keep
searching, and you will find. Keep knocking,
and the door will be opened to you.

Matthew 7:7

I cry aloud to God,
aloud to God, and He will hear me.

Psalm 77:1

The LORD is near all who call out to Him,
all who call out to Him with integrity.
He fulfills the desires of those who fear Him;
He hears their cry for help and saves them.

Psalm 145:18-19

You will petition Him,
and He will hear you. . . .
Light will shine on your ways.

Job 22:27a, 28b

Be gracious to me, Lord,
for I call to You all day long.
Bring joy to Your servant's life,
since I set my hope on You, Lord.
For You, Lord, are kind and ready to forgive,
abundant in faithful love
to all who call on You.

Psalm 86:3-5

A Hunger for Prayer

O God, You are my God;
   I eagerly seek You.
My soul thirsts for You;
   my body faints for You in a land
   that is dry, desolate, and without water.
So I gaze on You in the sanctuary
   to see Your strength and Your glory.
My lips will glorify You
   because Your faithful love is better than life.
So I will praise You as long as I live;
   at Your name, I will lift up my hands.
You satisfy me as with rich food;
   my mouth will praise You with joyful lips.

Psalm 63:1-5

*I know the Bible is inspired because
it finds me at greater depths of my
being than any other book.*
    —*Samuel Taylor Coleridge*

Come and see the works of God;
His acts toward mankind
are awe-inspiring. . . .
Come and listen, all who fear God,
and I will tell what He has done for me.
I cried out to Him with my mouth,
and praise was on my tongue.
If I had been aware of malice in my heart,
the Lord would not have listened.
However, God has listened;
He has paid attention
to the sound of my prayer.
May God be praised!
He has not turned away my prayer
or turned His faithful love from me.

Psalm 66:5, 16-20

A Hunger for Prayer

Call on Me in a day of trouble;
I will rescue you, and you will honor Me.
Psalm 50:15

Even before they call, I will answer;
while they are still speaking, I will hear.
Isaiah 65:24

How happy is the man
who has put his trust in the LORD
and has not turned to the proud
or to those who run after lies!
LORD my God, You have done many things—
Your wonderful works and Your plans for us;
none can compare with You.
If I were to report and speak of them,
they are more than can be told.
Psalm 40:4-5

But as for me, I will watch for the LORD;
I will wait for the God who saves me.
My God will hear me.
Micah 7:7

A Burden for Others

Being Selfish Is So Easy, and So Unsatisfying

Now finally, all of you should be like-minded and sympathetic, should love believers, and be compassionate and humble, not paying back evil for evil or insult for insult but, on the contrary, giving a blessing, since you were called for this, so that you can inherit a blessing.

1 Peter 3:8-9

"Everything is permissible," but not everything builds up. No one should seek his own good, but the good of the other person.

1 Corinthians 10:23b-24

If a brother or sister is without clothes and lacks daily food, and one of you says to them, "Go in peace, keep warm, and eat well," but you don't give them what the body needs, what good is it?

James 2:15-16

But when you give to the poor, don't let your left hand know what your right hand is doing, so that your giving may be in secret. And your Father who sees in secret will reward you.

Matthew 6:3-4

Therefore, through Him let us continually offer up to God a sacrifice of praise, that is, the fruit of our lips that confess His name. Don't neglect to do good and to share, for God is pleased with such sacrifices.

Hebrews 13:15-16

Render true justice; show faithful love and compassion to one another. Do not oppress the widow or the orphan, the stranger, or the poor, and do not plot evil in your hearts against one another.

Zechariah 7:9b-10

All bitterness, anger and wrath, insult and slander must be removed from you, along with all wickedness. And be kind and compassionate to one another, forgiving one another, just as God also forgave you in Christ.

Ephesians 4:31-32

Carry one another's burdens; in this way you will fulfill the law of Christ.

Galatians 6:2

For where envy and selfish ambition exist, there is disorder and every kind of evil. But the wisdom from above is first pure, then peace-loving, gentle, compliant, full of mercy and good fruits, without favoritism and hypocrisy.

James 3:16-17

A Burden for Others

The one who despises his neighbor sins,
but whoever shows kindness
to the poor will be happy.

Proverbs 14:21

The one who oppresses the poor
insults their Maker, but one who
is kind to the needy honors Him.

Proverbs 14:31

A generous person will be enriched,
and the one who gives a drink
of water will receive water.

Proverbs 11:25

*I read my Bible to know what people
ought to be doing, and my newspaper
to know what they are doing.*
—*John Henry Newman*

Promises for a Living Faith

Is this not the fast that I would choose:
   To break the chains of wickedness,
   to untie the ropes of the yoke,
   to set the oppressed free,
   and to tear off every yoke?
Is it not to share your bread with the hungry,
   to bring the poor and homeless one
   into your house, to clothe the naked
   when you see him, and not to turn
   your backs on your own flesh and blood?
Then your light will appear like the dawn,
   and your recovery will come quickly.
Your righteousness will go before you,
   and the LORD's glory will be your rear guard.
At that time, when you call,
   the LORD will answer;
   when you cry out,
   He will say, "Here I am."

Isaiah 58:6-9a

A Burden for Others

Do nothing out of rivalry or conceit, but
in humility consider others as more important
than yourselves. Everyone should look out not
only for his own interests, but also for the
interests of others.

Philippians 2:3-4

Since you put away lying, speak the truth,
each one to his neighbor, because we are
members of one another. . . . No rotten talk
should come from your mouth, but only what
is good for the building up of someone in need,
in order to give grace to those who hear.

Ephesians 4:25, 29

Now may the God of peace, who brought
up from the dead our Lord Jesus—the great
Shepherd of the sheep—with the blood of the
everlasting covenant, equip you with all that
is good to do His will, working in us what is
pleasing in His sight, through Jesus Christ,
to whom be glory forever and ever.

Hebrews 13:20-21

A Need *for* Accountability

Whatever I Need to Do to Stay True

I pray that your participation in the faith may become effective through knowing every good thing that is in us for the glory of Christ.

For I have great joy and encouragement from your love, because the hearts of the saints have been refreshed through you, brother.

Philemon 6-7

How good and pleasant it is
   when brothers can live together! . . .
For there the LORD has appointed
   the blessing—life forevermore.

Psalm 133:1, 3b

Therefore, brothers, stand firm and hold to
the traditions you were taught, either by our
message or by our letter. May our Lord Jesus
Christ Himself and God our Father, who has
loved us and given us eternal encouragement
and good hope by grace, encourage your hearts
and strengthen you in every good work and
word.

2 Thessalonians 2:15-17

Let us hold on to the confession of our hope
without wavering, for He who promised is faithful. And let us be concerned about one another
in order to promote love and good works, not
staying away from our meetings, as some habit-
ually do, but encouraging each other, and all
the more as you see the day drawing near.

Hebrews 10:23-25

A friend loves at all times,
 and a brother is born for a difficult time.
Proverbs 17:17

A man with many friends
 may be harmed, but there is a friend
 who stays closer than a brother.
Proverbs 18:24

I am a friend to all who fear You,
 to those who keep Your precepts.
Psalm 119:63

The wounds of a friend are trustworthy.
Proverbs 27:6a

It is better to listen to rebuke from a wise person
 than to listen to the song of fools.
Ecclesiastes 7:5

Teach me, and I will be silent.
 Help me understand what I did wrong.
Job 6:24

A Need for Accountability

The one who says he is in the light but hates his brother is in the darkness until now. The one who loves his brother remains in the light, and there is no cause for stumbling in him.

1 John 2:9-10

Anyone who ignores instruction despises himself, but whoever listens to correction acquires good sense.

Proverbs 15:32

We read the Bible to be fed. We read it to be converted, to be strengthened, to be taught, to be rebuked, to be counseled, to be comforted.

—Richard Foster

How happy is the man
  who does not follow
  the advice of the wicked,
  or take the path of sinners,
  or join a group of mockers!
Instead, his delight
  is in the LORD's instruction,
  and he meditates on it day and night.
He is like a tree planted
  beside streams of water
  that bears its fruit in season
  and whose leaf does not wither.
  Whatever he does prospers. . . .
For the LORD watches over
  the way of the righteous,
  but the way of the wicked
  leads to ruin.

Psalm 1:1-3, 6

A Need for Accountability

Watch out, brothers, so that there won't be in any of you an evil, unbelieving heart that departs from the living God.

But encourage each other daily, while it is still called today, so that none of you is hardened by sin's deception. For we have become companions of the Messiah if we hold firmly until the end the reality that we had at the start.

Hebrews 3:12-14

Love must be without hypocrisy. Detest evil; cling to what is good. Show family affection to one another with brotherly love. Outdo one another in showing honor.

Romans 12:9-10

May the God of endurance and encouragement grant you agreement with one another, according to Christ Jesus, so that you may glorify the God and Father of our Lord Jesus Christ with a united mind and voice.

Therefore accept one another, just as the Messiah also accepted you, to the glory of God.

Romans 15:5-7

A Passion for Living

Life with Him Is the Only Life I Want

Blessed be the God and Father of our Lord
Jesus Christ. According to His great mercy,
He has given us a new birth into a living hope
through the resurrection of Jesus Christ from
the dead, and into an inheritance that is imper-
ishable, uncorrupted, and unfading, kept in
heaven for you, who are being protected by
God's power through faith for a salvation that
is ready to be revealed in the last time.

1 Peter 1:3-5

Dear friends, we are God's children now, and what we will be has not yet been revealed. We know that when He appears, we will be like Him, because we will see Him as He is. And everyone who has this hope in Him purifies himself just as He is pure.

1 John 3:2-3

The hope of the righteous is joy, but the expectation of the wicked comes to nothing.

Proverbs 10:28

I keep the LORD in mind always.
   Because He is at my right hand,
   I will not be defeated.
Therefore my heart is glad, and my spirit
   rejoices; my body also rests securely.
For You will not abandon me to Sheol;
   You will not allow Your
   Faithful One to see the Pit.
You reveal the path of life to me;
   in Your presence is abundant joy;
   in Your right hand are eternal pleasures.

Psalm 16:8-11

If we have placed our hope in Christ for this life only, we should be pitied more than anyone.

1 Corinthians 15:19

For we too were once foolish, disobedient, deceived, captives of various passions and pleasures, living in malice and envy, hateful, detesting one another. But when the goodness and love for man appeared from God our Savior, He saved us—not by works of righteousness that we had done, but according to His mercy, through the washing of regeneration and renewal by the Holy Spirit.

Titus 3:3-5

For when you were slaves of sin, you were free from allegiance to righteousness. And what fruit was produced then from the things you are now ashamed of? For the end of those things is death.

But now, since you have been liberated from sin and become enslaved to God, you have your fruit, which results in sanctification—and the end is eternal life!

Romans 6:20-22

A Passion for Living

We have obtained access by faith into this grace in which we stand, and we rejoice in the hope of the glory of God. And not only that, but we also rejoice in our afflictions, because we know that affliction produces endurance, endurance produces proven character, and proven character produces hope. This hope does not disappoint, because God's love has been poured out in our hearts through the Holy Spirit who was given to us.

Romans 5:2b-5

The Bible is the truest utterance that ever came by alphabetic letters, through which, as through a window divinely opened, all men can look into the stillness of eternity and discern in glimpses their far-distant, long-forgotten home.
—Thomas Carlyle

Listen! I am telling you a myst
We will not all fall asleep,
but we will all be changed,
in a moment, in the twinkling of an eye,
at the last trumpet. . . .
Now when this corruptible
is clothed with incorruptibility,
and this mortal is clothed with immortality,
then the saying that is written will take place:
"Death has been swallowed up in victory."
O Death, where is your victory?
O Death, where is your sting?
Now the sting of death is sin,
and the power of sin is the law.
But thanks be to God,
who gives us the victory
through our Lord Jesus Christ!
1 Corinthians 15:51-52a, 54-57

A Passion for Living

So if you have been raised with the Messiah, seek what is above, where the Messiah is, seated at the right hand of God. Set your minds on what is above, not on what is on the earth.

For you have died, and your life is hidden with the Messiah in God. When the Messiah, who is your life, is revealed, then you also will be revealed with Him in glory.

Colossians 3:1-4

For the grace of God has appeared, with salvation for all people, instructing us to deny godlessness and worldly lusts and to live in a sensible, righteous, and godly way in the present age, while we wait for the blessed hope and the appearing of the glory of our great God and Savior, Jesus Christ.

Titus 2:11-13

Now may the God of hope fill you with all joy and peace in believing, so that you may overflow with hope by the power of the Holy Spirit.

Romans 15:13

*Look for these other Bible Promise books
to give to the special people in your life.*

Bible Promises for Mom
0-8054-2732-5

Bible Promises for Dad
0-8054-2733-3

**Bible Promises for
the Graduate**
0-8054-2741-4

**Bible Promises for
My Teacher**
0-8054-2734-1

Available in August 2003
Bible Promises for Kids 0-8054-2740-6
Bible Promises for Teens 0-8054-2739-2
Bible Promises for New Believers 0-8054-2742-2
Bible Promises for New Parents 0-8054-2738-4